Cover Art by ScienceImages
Author Photo by Caroline Yoder

The font used is Bookman Old Style and Book Antiqua
The cover font is Open Sans Light

Gnashing Teeth Publishing
242 East Main Street
Norman AR 71960
www.GnashingTeethPublishing.com

Printed in the United States of America

ISBN 979-8-9875694-0-5

Library of Congress Control Number: 2023945199

Fiction: Poetry

Gnashing Teeth Publishing First Edition

Praise for *Shared Blood*

Reading Luke Wortley is like staring into an M.C. Escher drawing, trying to figure out the origins, finding stairways as layers and echoes of what is absent. In Wortley's work, it is vital to understand how we rise up and build from loss, longing, and memory. This is a stunning, necessary collection. Bravo and welcome to this exciting prose poet.

Jose Hernandez Diaz, author of *The Fire Eater* and *Bad Mexican, Bad American.*

Shared Blood, the transfused and transforming new book by Luke Wortley, might just be William Wordsworth's and Russell Edson's sage and sanguine, Romantic and Expressionistic love child. The prose poems, a whole brooding passel of children being fathers to men, are engorged with gorgeous grotesqueries and all the tense tenses of time being too much with us. They whisper and whistle, sing and scat hemostatic hymns that suture and staunch the ruptured bleeding heartbreaks of all those hearts leaping to all those tympanic and tragic ups, all those known unknowns now known.

Michael Martone, author of *Plain Air: Sketches from Winesburg, Indiana* and *The Complete Writings of Art Smith, The Bird Boy of Fort Wayne, Edited by Michael Martone*

Luke Wortley's *Shared Blood* is a cohesive and connected collection of prose poems that see-saw between becoming a father while dealing with an estranged father of your own. Blending dream logic with the achingly real, *Shared Blood* presents Midwestern family life with a surrealist tilt of reality where everything is slightly sideways. In a world where staircases are made of hands and milk pours out of eyes, this is a book of lips and teeth and bones and bourbon. Ghosts and confessions and love and grief. Gutting, heart-wrenching paragraphs packed with absence. A city in a stomach, a sunflower sprouting out of a phone.

Ben Niesposziany, author of *No Farther than the End of the Street*
When I think of the prose poem, I think of a sacred space in which the real and the surreal can safely cohabitate, where strangeness can unfurl through small snippets of life like a red carpet. Luke Wortley's *Shared Blood* is a gorgeous and imaginative exemplar of how the prose poem can help us process difficult realities. The speaker of these poems moves seamlessly between reality and dreamscape, between the pain of being an estranged son and the anxiety of navigating new fatherhood. In order to break the cycle of trauma, to disinherit a legacy of lovelessness, the speaker searches frantically for a way to stop "slow-playing [his] own life." In this collection, Wortley steps through the portal of the prose poem again and again, ready to face the unknown that awaits on the other side.

Taylor Byas, author of *Bloodwarm* and *I Done Clicked My Heels Three Times*

Shared Blood
Prose Poems

Luke Wortley

For my mother.

I was the world in which I walked, and what I saw
Or heard or felt came not but from myself;
And there I found myself more truly and more strange.

Wallace Stevens

Contents

I

Expecting

When I open my front door, I see that the porch has turned into a clutch of eggs. All of them dumb and round and nestled tightly, packed in like pebbles on a drive. I'm afraid to step out and see what the temperature actually feels like other than a swipe of my hands, fingers slipping through the frigid air. I'm a mess. I don't know how to care for these eggs, how to keep them warm. The first gauzy drips of snow lean on the breeze like lace. I can't care for them all. Even so, I grab all the blankets in the house, pause at the door, and toss them. The wind screeches to life, and they land haphazardly in a pile some feet away, useless. It's too far to jump over all these eggs, and the temperature is dropping. Then, I feel my skin coming undone, the bonds decoupling from tendon and bone. I'm nearly blown away as I stretch and transform into a mantle of flesh. All of me stretches, out of necessity to cover the porch. Under me, I hear the whispering cries giving way to the quiet stupefaction of the entire nest.

Cry

When he's born, there is silence and there are wires. The beeping whine of machines and the stale odor of latex. Not long after, we're in the hot breath of the NICU, and the first scream blooms like a wound. Lightning quick: the way it unhinges my ear, undoes the surgical calm of night. I'm amazed by the use of breath, the way it careens in all of us, this storm in our son's mouth. I marvel at the tremulous nature of his gasp, the laborious intake. Each time it delays, I freeze, delve deeper into the porous stone of my wavering heart. I take my wife's hand, and we watch the monitor zip and undulate. I'm aware of the sudden lack of wind in the room, the cold embrace of sterile gloves as more thunder ripples from his mouth, sending us for cover as we brace for the coming quiet.

The Early Days

The whole world's oceans have turned to milk, and I'm wearing a t-shirt with a milk carton on it. There's milk in the horses' troughs and milk bottles littering the streets. There are milk stains on every mustache and loggers are quitting their jobs to work dairy farms. There are milk floods and milk rain, an anti-milk coalition, milk lobbyists. Milk in the clouds and milk in vending machines like it always was, except it's more popular than ever. Milk on my tongue. Milk droplets clinging to your knees and milk soothing our aching bones. There is life in the milk, too, and milk is life. There is milk running out of my eyes like tears and milk replacing bullets in guns. The opposite of fire is not water. It's milk. Milk drowns and sustains, leaks out of our son's mouth. There is milk on canvas. Milk evaporated, nestled in cans. And there is a childhood consumed with hunger, a want so deep, coiled in the waking hours of these first nights.

Sunflower

There were mass blackouts across the state. Rolling waves of loss, lights out. The rain came down with abandon, the river rising. We couldn't charge our phones, but my father called for the first time in nearly five years. I saw the word Dad flash on the screen, felt my stomach turn, the lilting waves of resistance starting to pinpoint themselves in my fingers. And yet there was a stooping desire to answer, to see what he wanted. We'd recently had a kid, and it was hard. Two weeks in the NICU and endless stretches of worrying about breath. Our son had been home for three weeks before my father finally called, and it was in the middle of this storm. It went to voicemail. The storm careened through the blotchy sky above, and I sat there watching the battery drain, watching the rivulets rise in the street. Eventually, the storm died, too, and the power came flickering on like a toe tap. I looked at my phone to see the screen cracked, a single sunflower blooming stupidly in the night. I plucked the stem from my screen and gave it to my wife, who laid it next to our son in the crib.

Near Miss

I'm taking my one-month-old son across the hall to change him when he jitters awake, kicks, and falls out of my arms. He tumbles into the dark. Before I can catch him, the house falls away and I'm on a shoreline watching him plunge from the slippery, cool sky. He falls back into my arms. The weight of him unimaginable mere moments ago. Then I'm holding him tight, the waves lapping at my feet, little crustaceans picking their way across the sand. I'm sinking ankle-deep into the sand with the rhythmic exodus of the water, listening to the hush. Salt ghosting the tongue. Relief creeping into my bones, curling off the terror of absence, the briefest of moments when he was gone. I hold him until the wind picks up and rushes in the tang of morning, the sky changing to bloody hues on the breeze. Then he's gone again, and I'm out treading in open water with only the thinnest memory of his cries. As I swim back toward shore, I hear my wife's voice on the swells, calling out to ask what's the matter.

Church

I could start with landing in bed with bourbon on the breath. The five-year plan and rebuild. The countless phone calls and sports texts. I could start with the time when my father and I flew together over the lake, how we shrunk down and climbed on top of a pair of swans. I could start with a willowy set of arms searching for embrace after five years of silence. I could start with the fact that this is all shadowed want and desire stretching over an imperfect stomach. I could start with staring in the mirror, with being bent over the toilet, fingers in the back of my mouth. But instead, the real starting point is the shallow culvert outside the church where he confronted me. Where the words flew out loud and thick. Thunder overhead. It starts with the rejection of his marriage, the quickening of the distance between us as the other woman looked on.

Four Wheeler

Dad's want coiled in bone, ready to spring out of a ribbed throat. Bleating desire ripping the air. Come for me and take me. Or retreat, find a way out and never come back, lick up the ounces of bourbon spilt and consumed. There will be calcified torment on the son's collarbone, dusting the little indentation of skin stretched taut. There will be a slinking memory of fist and shout, pummel and whine. You are my best friend, so you tell me. I've forgotten the exact intonation of the ice clinking in your glass but can still remember the slight edge of your cries that night you broke down and took the four-wheeler out, drunk, hurtling toward the barn. I remember the way you hit the divot in the yard and lost control of the handlebars, the way your body went limp as it crackled through the night air and landed with the softest of thuds on the bluegrass. The four-wheeler came to a restful stop as you laid there, barren. Swaying on the hot breeze, your shoulders moving on-time, one-two. Fescue clinging to your jeans. You broke the family that night. You broke the ineffable bond of the son, the tether to your constant refrains that kept me slow-playing my own life so that I could render everything in your name, prostrate myself before the altar of your approval. And I find that, now, since my wedding – the last time I heard your voice – I'm ready to put down that want and let it fester in your mouth.

Tumbler

I noticed that my tumbler glasses in my cabinet have all started to disappear. One by one, they're gone. Next, the spoons go, and then our shot glasses, followed by all the supply of lemonade at the grocery store. On the news, there's a global lemon shortage, interviews with silverware makers. They seem to have no memory of spoons whatsoever. But the tumbler glasses story never airs. After the tumblers are gone, our coffee cups vanish as well. I wonder how my father would deal with the crisis, as he was always poised in the recliner on the edge of sleep, his own tumbler filled with bourbon and lemonade tilting in his worn hands. The lilting scent of his cocktail playing in the roof of my own mouth. His jerking nods as he tried to avoid falling into darkness for the night, the ice melting silently. Grunts leaking out of his throat. My mother gently prying the tumbler from his grip and holding her breath.

Bones

Bright bones littering the cave floor, picked clean. Smoking bones in the firepit on the back porch. Bone-in. Bone-dry. Thin bones stirring the dregs of my cocktail. Finger bones on a string, twisting in the wind. Bone chimes. Whale bones forming a tunnel to the underworld. A tumor on a jawbone pressing deep into the flesh. Bony throats opening in the water, screaming for more. All the sweeping bones under the willow tree. Your teeth – the outside bones – floating on the southern breeze toward the cavernous maw of a combine. Yellow bones buried in dirt. Bone in your hand like a club, ready to break more bones. Prickly bones at the elbow, the ass, ankle beneath guilty skin of the other woman your father left your mother for. There are too many bones. Roll them bones, try your luck. Check out the crow perched on the skull, pecking the face bones of your forgotten ancestor. There are bones piled beneath still more bones. Bones in your chest, stretching. Bones in the recesses of memory holding up what you have left of your father.

Footsweep

And yet I crave the slippage of clavicle, the resurrected din of mandible jutting beside a wrecked fist. I'm a little hazy on the specifics of a smoky chest, a billowing set of teeth strewn across the lawn. Of fatherhood, I must say there's a certain set of circumstances that come bearing down at full tilt as soon as a slender digit slices open or a tight scream rumbles into the space between humbled breaths, a threaded submission in my throat. I find that it's hardly worth the weight of knees. Against the onslaught of the memory, I contort my stomach into an imperfect array of armored plates, try and deflect or simply lay prone on the bluegrass, stare at the twisting vertebrae of stars. I admit that I might be misremembering this time out in the yard when my feet got taken out, my father's arms sliding, his hands jeweled by moonlight – I should mention that I skipped the part where we'd been hammering back yowls of bourbon, throats kindled and spent roughing up the air in a storm of silence and a glaze of ethereal praise – to the point that it was a blinding spin of perpetuity when they came down on my chest and chin. Pinned to the soil, I still writhe to the beat of pummeling hands, to the bobbing of an Adam's apple taking a shot.

Goatman

My father is the goatman. Tonight, I undid myself in the evening air, managed to leave my body in fear of him chasing me, footsteps heavy and slick. His hooves and horns shadows in starlight. His horns came in during the divorce proceedings and never went away. They erupted seemingly overnight, arcing around the sides of his head, ending in grotesque, rounded tips. And I refused to acknowledge them for years, calling him and calling him and letting him prattle on about my mother before I finally saw the truth and ran. Now he's caught me, the stench of him weighing on the slight wind. I'm floating above myself as he approaches my body lying crooked in the bluegrass. He picks me up, my arms dangling, carved by starlight. I'm screaming into the cicada song bombing over the next ridge, trying to wake myself, to return to the fight. I see him lean his goat face gingerly to my chest and sniff. In my current form, I can still feel the breath of him, the buoyant breath of promise as he used to say to me, *You're my best friend. You know that, right?* And I believed him. But no more. No more cloudy swindles and drunken reassurance. Now, I'm the spirit and he's the monster. My body swaying in his arms – a parody of how I hold my son and carry him across the hall to bed. There we are there, me, my mind, and this monster, the night pressing close, and all I can think of is survival and repentance. I know I won't get both, so I dive back in, reel through the pain splitting the sides of my head as I struggle in his arms yet again.

Fencepost

I'll start with the son, the one who watched his father's arms uncurl in sunlight, watched his calves pulse when he dug a new hole for a fencepost all those years ago. I'll start with the father, the one who uncurled his arms in broad daylight just to show his son what he expected, who sank the posthole digger into the earth as though driving a stake through the monster's heart. Either way, what I have is a picture of acquiescence and militance, a portrait of relationship bound to a single moaning dread. What I have is something that I can't divorce from the I, from the we, from the father and son, the son who has become the father. When he's moved out, left my mother, and gone to live with another family, I drive back down to the house, get out and walk to that fencepost, take in the solidity of it, the darkness of the paint. Heat boiling in my throat. I can see the imperfections, all the nooks and crannies of labor and wear, of callous dismissal and bourbon-laced shouts followed by caresses, repeating, *You're my best friend, you know that, right?* I can see the shadow of my father's arms reaching, looking to clobber me all over again, this time from somewhere else.

Angel

I can hold an angel in my palms only for so long, but my father could do it forever. He could lock it up with his thin fingers, wings wilting there in his hands before he let it go like a firefly, flashing a confident smile.

For me, the angel always escaped, turned and laughed at me. All I could feel was shame. But I always gave chase, hunting down the little beast, searching for the slightest hint of disturbance on the breeze. I never knew how small angels were until I tried to hold them, but laughter booms from such a tiny body.

This time, I've caught one that got away. I try to mimic my father's locked grip, can feel the miniscule wings brushing my calluses, the tiny hands pressing on mine. I hold with all I have, the strength of the angel testing my palms and fingers. I press harder until the movement ceases, the voice fizzles. I keep pressing, trying to be just like my father. When I open my fingers to let it free, I find nothing there. The breeze sweeps over my shoulder as though tapping me, willing me to turn around and look.

Beast

You can find the son at the back of a father's throat if you're listening. If you're listening, it's possible that you might hear the father's complaints, the undertones of regret. Regret the self-effacing need to file down to the skin, to wear your wounds so red and open, even beneath your clothes. Beneath your clothes, your soul is a flight risk. Risk the absolute worst when it comes to immolation and renovation, the way it all comes crashing down in a spiral of lips and teeth. Lips and teeth the visible things that communicate want. The visible things that communicate want bleeding out on the ground. On the ground, a slavering beast. Beast is what they call you, if you're looking hard enough. If you're looking hard enough, you can find the origin of the father. The father who prayed to the liquor cabinet and drove a tractor through the fields under the stars. Under the stars, a ceaseless blowing wind. Wind-whipped rain on the first day of school. The first day of school, the discovery of the other woman, the other family, a Mercedes Benz with hail damage on the hood, the screaming match and the leaving. Leaving, when practiced, is easy.

Language

For the first time in a very long time, I woke up to a voicemail from my father. But it was in a language I couldn't understand. It sounded vaguely like German, but I knew it wasn't actually German. So I downloaded every app I could find and tried to type it out in English phonetically. Nothing worked. The more I searched the more mesmerizing it became. Each syllable was a diaphanous cutlet of language, a tear in my heart, nectar dripping into my ears. I listened to it so much that, eventually, I thought I could understand it. What it said was, Please, stop. I'm here. Over and over.

Patrilineal

The other night, I tilted the bottle over the edge of the bonfire and watched the smoke plume into my dead grandad's form, the one I never knew, the one who survived two train crashes and a hive of yellow jackets but succumbed to blood poisoning. He motioned, and I followed him to the creekbed. As we walked, he told me of a time when he buried his own shadow, how his fingers sprouted up, and he jammed them back down. He told me how it struggled, how this first death was to prove to his own father he could stomach the act. When I asked him why he did it, he said he had to prepare for the vehemence of the land, the inevitability of its thirst. He said his own father spoke in thunderous gulps and tinny sounds sloshing in the bottle. They said he never was much of a talker. I beg to differ. Frogsong lay on the air like a veil as we walked back up the valley. Sliced with moonlight, we kept wandering, him stooping in a smoky wave, sliding through the shimmer. Another night, tilting another bottle, my father told me of his first kill. A squirrel jittering up a tree, the crazy thwack of a pellet to the back of its twitchy head. He said it stiffened and fell, the grass stroked with garnet as it flopped and squealed. So I asked my granddad about that, felt my throat tighten as his mouth opened. I was expecting some defense, perhaps a winding apology. What came out was a train whistle hammering the breeze, blowing over me in a dry heat. His breath loud and furious, brushed with the tang of shared blood.

II

Box

I have all my memories of my father in a cardboard box. I take them with me wherever I go and take a few out at a time, let them fall to the floor. The time he screamed in my corner at a judo match while I writhed with a broken elbow. A wild chase around the yard ending up with me on my back in the bluegrass staring up at the stars. A compilation of occasions with him slurring *You're my best friend, you know that?* Him being told by his friends over and over to stop using that type of language at the dinner table in front of the kids. When I place them back in the box, I can taste the sour hint of bourbon on the back of my tongue, can feel the ghost of his hand on the back of my neck, still ache for the cleaving clarity of his voice.

Birthday

On my thirtieth birthday, I discover a pain in my jaw. It kicks the living joy out of the entire day. I go upstairs and lie in bed, listen to the somnolent hum of the guests downstairs buzzing over themselves with tilting cups. My wife comes up and asks if I'm okay. It is a milestone birthday, after all. Thirty years old. Three years since my father and I last spoke. Years being the measurement of our distance, now. Years in the gut, remembered in the coiled muscle. It feels like there's a miniature planet underneath my back left molar. It whirls and dips in the socket, pulling me into the hot panic of hurt. I toss and turn, take a pull of beer, think of his absence, the spinning. My mouth feels full of starlight, brimming with gravity. Cold and dry. The party downstairs droning like wind through the thistle, distant as a museum. The next day, when the party's over, I go to the dentist, who refers me to an oral surgeon. It turns out to be a bone infection, and then I have a peripherally inserted central catheter sluicing antibiotics directly into my heart for six weeks. The insertion point, just where the elbow bends, itches all the time. My mind is constantly windswept as I crawl into bed. Eating becomes a fear. My father does eventually text me, and it's a link to a tweet from my favorite hockey team, a highlight from nearly two years ago.

The King and the Prince

There once was a king and a prince. The prince was a flirtatious lad with a penchant for running around the kingdom shirtless, avoiding his guards, and generally having a good time. The king was a surly ruler who always weighed his choices methodically with his advisors and tended to his queen with perfunctory grace.

The kingdom prospered, but the king was also known to think dark thoughts and drink too much mead in the late hours, droning on about his son's lack of interest in ruling. It was known to make the guards gossip about the future of the realm. The prince, on the rare occasion he was home in the castle, would drink as well and lament his lack of interest in ruling, his desire to roam and avoid his father.

When the king died and the prince took over, the kingdom went into economic tailspin, as the prince – now king, but we'll still call him the prince – spent a fortune on the funeral and grieved so conspicuously that he neglected all financial responsibility. Nobody understood the prince's grief, as the two never seemed particularly close, but the prince wore a black cloak and incessantly polished his black boots for years before he finally took a tour of the kingdom at the behest of his advisors, some of whom had grown quite old and wizened, and saw the ruin of his domain.

The prince refused the court's proposals of marriage, and he ruled from his bed in his solar, staring at the smooth stone. Eventually, the advisors were able to stabilize the kingdom while the prince still grieved. He cried and heaved, his soul leaking out in rippling sobs bit by bit until one day, he realized he could no longer cry. So, he set about attending council meetings, getting up at a decent hour, letting color back into his wardrobe.

The prince ruled with ruthless efficiency after he cried his last tear, and the coffers filled yet again, fuller than they'd ever been under his father's rule. The prince banned public displays of grief, outlawed funerals, and even went so far as to decree crying in public a crime punishable by banishment from the realm.

Eventually, the memories of his father returned, and he still found he was unable to cry, unable to summon even the most private of tears. And when the memories returned, he got up, walked out of his solar, through the great halls of his castle, and into the wood, never to be seen again.

Elevator

I'm on an elevator when it stops between floors. The metallic swirl of losing purchase always on the back burner, the fear of falling fresh as aloe. There are other sounds as well: breath, popping knuckles, frantic clicking of buttons like beetles skittering. It's just me in the elevator, but the feeling is there that my father has infiltrated the space, laid claim to this confinement. I sense his broad chest and pulsing shoulders, the sharpness of his stubbled jaw. I sit down in the corner and wait for help to arrive, my thoughts jostling each other with the spirit of him. I go back to the last time we spoke. At a chain restaurant in Indianapolis. He wanted the woman he'd cheated on mom with to be called grandma. I remember the tines of our forks dry, the ice in our cocktails slipping past each other like cells as my wife and I got up with our infant son before any food could arrive. Just then, he's opening the doors and pulling me into the innards of the building, and we're bounding up the shaft toward the roof, hurtling toward a blistering ball of light. A whirring sound fills my ears as we ascend, hand in hand toward the glow. When we're there, the ball of light swallows him whole and implodes. My pocket buzzes with easy ferocity while I float around the intricate systems and endless metal. I pull my phone out to see a text from him, a link to an article about my favorite football team. I get these texts from him once a year – some disembodied sports highlight – and this is the time, just after my rescue. But perhaps I'd been better off waiting.

Monster

My son and I are on a hike. I'm tying my son's shoes when a monster crawls out of the woods and devours us whole. We barely avoid the teeth on the way down its gullet, slipping painfully into the cavernous stomach. We wander around for hours until we hear a rumbling above. Throughout the next few days, the monster swallows another father and son followed by still more pairs of fathers and sons. Until we populate the bottom of the stomach and whisper greetings to each other, decide that, yes, this is our life now, and we'd better make the most of it. So, we build a city in the stomach and listen for the soft rumbling here and there that means our population has grown. On my way to the grocery store, I befriend another father named Marcus, who affectionately changes my name every time I see him in the weeks to come. I never correct him. We share beer and watch our sons play together in the park. It suddenly occurs to us that we haven't heard the rumbling since we met. We awkwardly part ways after a few looks upward toward the mammoth throat. The city goes quiet, all the traffic stops, and the slow silence sets in. Nobody talks for weeks after that, and everyone stays in their spacious, modern apartments, not venturing out except to go to the store, and even then, everything is done quietly, the only blips of sound ringing out of the cash registers. The quiet drags on, and eventually we all forget each other's names. One day, we hear the rumbling above and cheer wildly.

Games

I'm playing board games with my son. He places a pawn on various action spaces, and a scraggly pile of wood appears next to his chair. I place mine, and a jar of pine resin pops up next to me on our ever-dwindling table as it gets cluttered with more stuff. We continue like this until we've amassed enough resources to build a house on a bed of river rock right there in our sitting room. When it's done, we have a sweaty look. Inside, there's a gleaming bowl of starlight, a family of fieldmice tapping away in synchronized dance, a gleaming tabernacle, my father's old work wardrobe. I walk through the closet with my son and check out the innards of the house, explore my father's wardrobe with curious abandon. We begin trying on shirts, slipping pants over our skinny legs. We're swimming in all his clothes, the giant. And then I find a t-shirt and a pair of gym shorts that fit perfectly. I whirl around to show my son, who looks frightened. I want to tell him that everything is okay, that the play here is just to let the costume be what it is.

Hoodie

I left my favorite hoodie at my father's house nearly five years ago. No other hoodie will do, and, trust me, I've tried. I've tried on every single other hoodie in the world. Pulled them out of the wash in great, damp ropes, slipped them over my head, stacked them a mile high, organized them by color and brand, made beds and napped in them. None of them compare to the tousled softness of my favorite hoodie – an unremarkable blue one with a university name stitched across the chest. I wonder if it's still there at my father's house with the other woman, if it's sitting folded neatly in hopes I might remember where they live and make it a habit to leave things there and come back on occasion to pick them up. If, maybe, I'll let him roll out his confessions when he hands it over, feel the pull of kindred. I speak in hypotheticals, as though I'm actually contemplating a return to that windswept house full of people who text me asking when I'll talk to my father again.

Orchids

My son asks me why I'm so obsessed with my father. His face a gleaming moon in the evening air as we sit on the back porch drinking lemonade. Mine with bourbon. All the ice melted. *I don't know*, I say. Fireflies around us dancing constellations. *Yes you do*, he says. The honest truth is that I don't know. We haven't spoken in seven years, not since my son was born. Maybe it's the strange occurrences on the way, the gliding exhalation of my breath laced with liquor, perhaps even just the uncanny bond of fatherhood, even from such a distance marked by time. I walk over to him, bend down to his eye level, and pull him into a hug. Between us, pressure, an unknowable want surfacing in my chest, a balloon of regret and need. Then he's choking, sputtering, coughing, disengaging from our embrace. A bouquet of orchids erupts from his mouth and settles wetly on the deck as he heaves in relief. Inside, I hear my wife singing as she cuts up a particularly fragrant onion. I look at my son, who looks back at me, down at the orchids, and laughs the most beautiful laugh.

Stairs

When I come home from work, I open the door and find the staircase is made of hands. Hands of all different shapes and colors, caught in different poses, tucked in together like leaves. I pluck one that seems roughly the same hue and size as mine, grasp its palm, and immediately break into a sweat. The palms are calloused in the way my father's hands were, and I find this to be towering, the memory of his touch. And when I'm ready to let go, the hand with my father's touch hangs on. I can't shake it loose. So, I end up carrying it around with me; it grasps even as I relax my grip. It stays there on my morning jogs. It clings to me as I try and drive through the winding suburbs, is present under the table when I'm eating dinner. The longer it stays, the heavier it gets, and soon my shoulder is strained all the time. My posture sinks. I learn to do everything with my opposite hand. It's been a year since we spoke, and the urge to find fire is constantly scraping at the back of my neck, creeping into my desire to burn the hand off or sear it there forever.

Ouroboros

I find myself in a political debate with a timber rattlesnake slithering out of the fescue. It asks me if I believe human beings should be afforded special privileges and rights based on their perceived sense of superior consciousness. I say I've never considered the question before, which is not true. I've contemplated many permutations of this question, just never in relation to snakes. The snake rears up pensively and shows its fangs. I can see a gossamer droplet glimmering on the tip of one of them. I don't recall now if it was the left or the right. Of course you haven't, says the snake, its voice uncannily similar to my father's. So, I ask him if he believes snakes are ultimately destined to eat their own tails. That's a wicked stereotype, he says, and I confess I can't answer his question without looking too much like an idiot. Just so, the snake turns and slithers away into the grass as I feel my jaw unhinge and my body contort toward my feet.

Hunting

I run the washer and transfer a load to the dryer. Then I go to the kitchen and pour myself a beer. It's around 4pm on a Tuesday, but I don't care. When the timer sounds, I open the door and out pops a yapping coyote. It rips through my house and tears up all my clothes, even the ones on my body. And so I'm walking through the house naked, looking at the devastation and swinging through the ethereal dark with a weight in my stomach as I keep on sipping. Then the air is full of coyotes snapping at the air outside. I look out a window, trying to cover myself, and see a whole pack of them loping about the yard. One pauses and looks at me with a sallow sort of expression. Aren't they supposed to be active at night? I finish my beer and pour another, the shuffling of my brain starting to dull a bit from the shock of having my clothes ripped off. I keep drinking and my thoughts turn to my father, who I haven't seen in nearly five years. I remember a time we went coyote hunting with a .45 and saw a sickly mother and her rabid pups curled up under a brush pile. I remember the sanguine swoop of his trigger finger, the bang. The world liquefied for a moment in the ringing aftermath as though everything were made of tears. I remember him standing there, wielding the pistol with reverence, handing it to me as he put on a pair of raw work gloves and began hauling the carcasses. I remember the weight of it in my hand as I take another sip, feel my stomach turn to forged metal and sink down into a chair. When I look out the window again, it's nearly dark, and I see the yard littered with a dozen skinny pelts.

Troll

My father came over and asked me to be his best man, and I said yes, even though I didn't want to. I didn't want to stand up there in church and smile. But I did. At the wedding, there was a woman handing out acorns and a troll in attendance. The troll cradled his acorn gently in his gargantuan hands and cried when he saw the bride, who I'd only known as the other woman. After the wedding, the troll trudged off into the woods wiping his amber eyes.

My father came over and asked me if my son will call the other woman grandma, and I said no. It was just my father and me in that room when he asked, and our breath was unbearably hot. We didn't speak again for five years. I did take a stroll in the woods, though, and I saw the troll tending to his oak sapling with a tenderness I didn't know existed.

Conversation

The father says, *You're my best friend. You know that, right?*

The son says, *Yeah, I know. You're mine, too.*

The father says, *I love you.*

The son says, *I love you, too.*

The father says, *More than anything in this world.*

The son says, *I know. Me too.*

The father says, *I need to tell you something.*

The son says, *Okay. What is it?*

The father says, *Please, just hear me out. I need you to know this isn't your fault.*

The son says, *I know.*

The father says, *I don't know what to do about it.*

The son says, *Me neither.*

The father says, *What would you do?*

The son says, *Don't ask me that.*

The father says, *Why not?*

The son says, *Because I'm not you.*

The father says, *Aren't you?*

Smoke

The father takes another drag on a cigarette but it hasn't shortened at all. He's in the garage and has told his son that he'll be back in after this smoke. He smokes furiously, fuming breath after breath. Inside, he knows his son is waiting. *How long now?* he wonders. He takes yet another drag, watching the frantic end light up with his breath. The garage fills with clouds of his smoke, and he's desperate to get back in, but this cigarette seems to have a magnetic hold on his hand, his arm moving robotically from his waist to his lips over and over. He looks out of the garage, sees the pop of heat lightning in the distance.

Father in War Time

Father as a self-portrait of his son, as a leaking gas can. Father in the hills overlooking a scream. It's a father-son time on the corroded playground. Then father on the father time loop scooping water into his hand. You can give the father a carrot and watch him turn it into something beautiful, can witness the shredded ribbons of his t-shirt fall on the yard. Father as a victim, as a tether ball wrapped around a pole. Forgotten streams of fatherhood winding their way to the river. Father with raised voice, with a large glass of bourbon. It's drink and argue time, father burnout time on the sizzling summer day back when the son might've still been amenable to correction.

The Son Holds

The son has an autopilot feature that lets him endure the father. The son is a brilliant tour de force in tolerance, a broken knee in homage to shattered statues. The son blinking through tears. About to leave, he turns at the door and decides not to shout. The son may have a messianic complex he inherited from his father, may decide to jettison it someday with careful reflection and if he meets the right people. An immaculate smile rippling through the yells. The son as fishing line dipping beneath the surface, as a gleaming scale on a picnic table. Lately, it's a string of cut-your-losses kind of nights, a collection of apologies and defenses littering the floor and spattered with accidental blood relation. To the son, it's a time to cower and a time to stand up. To the son, it's all the same.

Portrait of a Father

The father is a war hero, a mechanic of souls, the one-time runner-up and the former champ in his son's eyes. Is a calloused dictator on the run brandishing a cigar and growing a gnarly beard. Is supposed to be hunting down a way to say he's sorry. Is supposed to be tossing a ball in the yard, raking leaves. Can be thought of as the antidote and the poison, a curlicue of regret laced with ancestry. Is a gleaming spark on the end of a stick poking out of the fire. Is crashing through the undergrowth and getting a rash. Can also be the plaintiff in this case, the accuser of dread and separation, the aggressor looking for an opening. The father is a husk of drunken stupor charging around the living room. Is a neglected little pinprick in the night sky. Is supposed to be the descendent and the progenitor, the unwavering vessel of blood.

Portrait of a Son

The son is a scythe ripping through the grain, a ringing endorsement of inherited violence. Is nestled in the haunches of his father's legacy and careening through memory. Can be defined only by the vehemence of blood, the gorgeous wrapping of hands around an upper arm and the march to the fenceline. Is grieving his estranged father despite his wife's protestations and despite the fact that he's very much alive but just living with another family. Is undressing in the middle of the night and looking for something to hunt. Is drinking too much, hiding the filigreed remains of wanton sex and the too close utterances of the other, standing over the toilet with a finger down his throat. The son is the open wound, the intractable thirst for what's gone forever.

Confessions of the Father

I picked a fishing hook out of my son's hand and stemmed the small trickle of blood with my mouth. The frog song buried us in its sheen, the cattails singing old Catholic hymns. The fish jumped and rolled. I reached out and caught a bluegill, cut my own hand on its spines, sucked that wound, too.

<

I want to devour my son. I want him to consume me.

<

I've tried to write about my son, found the words would not come, and licked the page. It tasted of salted caramel.

<

On Holy Saturday, I found out that I could dissemble my limbs and rearrange them in any monstrous order I chose. I kept this knowledge from my family and never actually managed to pull myself apart, but I knew that I could. And it was terrible.

<

There is no son without the father.

<

I can't write more than ten lines at a time, and that fact has me stupefied. So I drink too much bourbon and settle into the haunches of a La-Z-Boy, thinking of the way my own father might have handled this latest disappointment, how his fingers would wrap around a tumbler just like this one, tilt it back. How he would cough due to a wrong swallow.

<

There's a tiny mountain under my bed. I worry it will keep growing and reach its true potential someday, split the bed in half. Then maybe I'll never see my wife and son again. I wonder how many months we'd spend hugging the base of the mountain, hopping over streams and pressing through endless sheets of pine needles. Outside, a coyote yips its crazed cantata. The springs of our mattress rumble under our weight.

<

I'm obsessed with throats.

<

I confess that grief isn't my strong suit. My strongest suit is self-loathing, and I wear it exceptionally well.

<

I repurposed a bunch of junk into a jetpack and took my sleeping son away into the air. We flew over Washington, D.C., Marseilles, Ankara, and Karachi, him asleep the entire time. I watched his eyelashes flutter as we passed through clouds, waved to the stock footage of flocks of birds flapping below. I returned home and put him back in bed before my wife ever knew we'd gone.

<

There is no father without the son.

<

When I found out I was bipolar, my life made a lot more sense, and all of a sudden the shadows in the corners of my eyes turned to dust.

<

I went to the store for the fifth time in a week and was the only person there. Every time I loaded something in the cart, a companion item that made no sense would appear next to it. I'd put in a bag of chips and coffee filters would show up. Tomatoes followed by a box of mechanical pencils. I tried to put everything back. But then I kept losing the item I was looking for in the first place. So I quit and walked outside. There was a TV reporting crew there for the local news. The microphones pressed in like a swarm of gigantic bugs. I was overwhelmed by the questions and jumped into the camera.

<

I'm slick with need.

<

I want to hollow out my own stomach and let it fly into the night. I want my son to know what kind of father I think I am and make sure he never finds out what kind of father I actually am. I want there to be a guardrail on the edge of desire and an endless supply of ice. I want all ramifications to be swept under the rug. I want a twittering parakeet who can mimic my son's voice. I want there to be an end to silence.

Confessions of the Son

Sometimes I think my father is gone. When this happens I wonder if I'm gone, too.

>

There is no father without the son.

>

I stood on a promontory naked and dared the wind to push me off. The wind was so frightened of my pelvis that it retreated and blew me back onto more solid ground. I cursed the wind for its garish show of strength and put my clothes back on. My father wouldn't have approved.

>

A dying star wandered into my bedroom. I reached out to shake its hand, and it wanted nothing to do with me. I told it how my father dragged me through the fescue and made me king of a patch of dirt, and it got teary-eyed. Great ribbons of galaxy dust spewed from its face, and I wrapped my arms around it, leaned in for a kiss.

>

The last woman I dated was afraid I'd leave her for a man who looked like my father.

>

I turned my hair into kindling for a bonfire, and it burned for an entire month. I never had to feed it anything else except my hair. But it was my father's hands who made the pile to begin with.

>

I kiss with cold breath. It's extremely off-putting until the tongue becomes accustomed, feels all the undulating pressure. From what my father has told me, this is normal.

>

When I look through old photographs on my phone, I find that my father isn't in any of them. There's just a smudge of color. Sometimes cyan, my son's favorite color. And when my son sees it, he looks at me with his sweeping gray eyes almost as if to ask, Is this what it all means? I keep scrolling, unwilling to acknowledge his questioning face. I move to more pictures of our old cat, the one we put down just before a storm dashed itself against our living room window. My wife's fingernails detach and flutter into the fireplace.

>

I confess there is too much to confess.

>

My tattoos are all moving to different parts of my body. My father has more tattoos than me, but I like mine better. Plus, they move.

>

When it snows, I hide under my desk and can't write because of the silence.

>

The first time I made myself throw up, a gleaming deer ricocheted out of my throat and plopped into the toilet. I lifted it up, water falling off its coat like cabochons. It pranced in my palm, waiting for the rut to begin.

>

There is no son without the father.

>

At night I consort with whales. I find the arcing bones irresistible. The wisdom of their solemn cries piercing and dark and filling. I want to destroy them. I want to be them. I want nothing more than to take my own whale form so that I can hate my body all over again.

>

If my father were to die before we reconnected, I think the world might stop spinning. There might be a cataclysmic silence brewing in my son's throat. There might be more cicadas than usual. There might be a loving embrace between my wife and me, a tightening of shoulders. There might be a few bricks missing, the structure precarious. There might be a ghoul running rampant through a suburban park. There might be all manner of detritus washing up on shores, on front porches. There might be bullet casings littering the parking lot of a grocery store. There might be occasion to get the grill out and have a massive cookout. There might be absolutely nothing at all.

III

Medicine

There is new medication swinging through veins on the heels of diagnosis. Bipolar II, ricocheting childhood acts of contrition, blown out bones of fatherhood. Trauma coiled in the stomach and searching for the identity of the son, clamoring for all the lost loves and apologies that need to be heard. It swirls in the rounded hollows of my brain and corrals the aching surges of a need to demolish something or other, to rectify impossible wrongs. It leaks out of my breath and soothes my wife, reinvigorates my son, who now knows which Daddy he's going to get. It's the flow of quotidian, the unrelenting grasp of what is actually there and not lurking in the corner or in the shadow of broken sleep. It's the controlled pours of bourbon into the shot glass, a finger dipped in for taste only. There is struggle and tug, pull and swallow, but there is also hope for something that resembles the real, the uninterrupted current of parenting without the urge to break down, to be caught out and calling the hotline. It's the promise of requited desire on the tip of a wet tongue and the stinging normalcy of living among the living, to become the father I never had.

Call

A dead cell phone. A voluminous skirt draped over a fence. A thousand used teabags lining a gravel drive. Fourteen clean chicken wing bones. A box containing the remains of our orange cat. The lunar curve of my wife's pregnant stomach. A god trapped behind my steepled fingers waiting for his day of vengeance. My father's filet knife, sharp and bedraggled with guts. My father's fingernails and flecks of skin from his hands littering the dashboard. Spit-washed baseballs in a green bucket. The protrusion of a wrist bone under long sleeves. A furtive nod. A pearl necklace lying abandoned in the fescue. A noiseless guitar. My father's ruined knuckles. A before and after. A sex stain on wrinkled sheets. The bottle of tawny liquid tilting into my throat. A pair of stilettos hanging from meat hooks. A crucifix with filigreed palms tucked behind it. The sting of sweat in the eyes while standing in the middle of a pasture. Clammy palms. A corrupt official screaming at a computer screen, wanting to know where the money is. Slick stones in my pockets. A fortune cookie torn in half and left on the coffee table. All this, and I'm still waiting for my father to call.

Pocket Square

A rolling breeze on fire. Several thousand mushrooms popping up overnight. A faded pile of magazines sitting on the staircase. A single Christmas light. A steady rise and fall of a baby's chest. The haunted room with the blue door. A collection bowl being passed around at mass. Garrulous shadows chatting away in the corner. A bird smashed into the windshield while driving 55mph on the state highway. A spider web strung up in the swing set out back. A promontory draped with moss. My father's jagged cursive on the front of a check. A bed in the middle of the woods with springs sticking out of it. The aberrant twittering of bats in the evening. Younger versions of ourselves manipulating the past so we never truly age. A beat so catchy you can't help but swing your hips and lick the night. Salt in the wound. A preoccupation with breath. The sallow sliver of moon cutting across the sky. A bottle of aloe vera. A lonesome barn with a red tin roof is towering in the middle distance. My father's gingham pocket square blooming from my coat pocket.

Dad's Weekend

The boy asks his dad why he cheated on Mom. It's Dad's weekend, and it's the first time the boy has been this frank. The boy is only eleven, so the dad doesn't really answer. Instead, the dad produces a cage with one hand, extending it with a perfunctory *I don't know*. Inside the cage is a twittering green parakeet. This is insufferable to the boy, who gets up and walks to his room. The click of the doorlatch dreamy and sweet. The dad, sitting there with the bird, thinks about thin bones, wet tongues tossing over each other. Despite himself, he feels a stirring. So he carries the cage to the boy's door, pauses, and sets it down before stalking off to the kitchen to pour a shot of bourbon. He focuses on the carefully stacked mail on the end of the dining room table, the closeness of the corners of paper, drinks. Sometime later, the son emerges as a full-grown man, face shimmering above a slick beard. All the while the bird is shiftily preening, shuffling through its feathers. The dad stares into the dregs of his glass, wonders how much time has passed. Then he watches the man pick up the cage and reach inside; watches the bird silently hop onto the man's finger, its head tilting wildly; watches the man take the bird to the window and set it on the sill before going to the kitchen where the dad is leaning against the countertop. The dad notices that the man is crying, but the dad's mind is clouded with drink. His skull a glittering cave. He stumbles back to the liquor cabinet and finds a second glass. Time to share, to come clean. Then a breeze comes through, and the father sees that the bird is gone, along with his son.

What Happens When We Die

The son asks, *Dad, what happens when we die?*

The dad says, *I'm not sure. Ask me when I die.*

The son says, *But you'll be dead.*

The dad asks, *Then how else will you find out?*

The son says, *By asking you now.*

The dad says, *Have a drink with me first.*

The son asks, *Am I old enough?*

The dad says, *Yes.*

The son says, *This stuff is awful. How do you do it?*

The dad says, *With practice.*

The son says, *Seriously.*

The dad asks, *What?*

The son asks, *What happens when we die?*

The dad asks, *You wanna know what I think?*

The son says, *Yes. More than anything.*

The dad says, *I think we coil into the song of the cicadas and only emerge to eat, proliferate, and die again. I firmly believe that, if I'm being honest, we glint on the shimmer of tears before we fall and are forgotten again. I think we live on in the heart monitors in the hospital and in the rush of water through underground caves. I think we melt at the bottom of these glasses and linger on the tongue of the living for just a few sour moments.*

The son asks, *You wanna know what I think?*

The dad says, *Yes. More than anything.*

The son says, *I think we become nothing and nothing becomes us.*

The dad says, *I think that's a sad thought.*

The son asks, *Why? What you said is way sadder.*

The dad asks, *How so?*

The son says, *Well, in your scenario, each time we're remembered it's fleeting. It passes in smoke from the tip of a cigarette, gone in the time it takes to finish the final drag. If what you said is true, our death is, as a fundamental datum, inconsequential as this drink. If what you said is true, we don't live on as you think we do. Our memory is around long enough only to cause hurt and then be forgotten.*

The dad says, *Wow.*

The son says, *I know.*

The dad says, *I never thought of it that way before.*

The son says, *Perhaps it's because you're convinced of the natural order of things. I, for one, have considered that I might die before you.*

The dad asks, *Why do you think that?*

The son says, *I don't necessarily think that. I've just considered the possibility.*

The dad asks, *But why?*

The son says, *I just imagine the world as a hapless, spinning yoyo, and at any time the thing can come unraveled, spin off into the void, you know?*

The dad says, *I think so. So, what do you wish happened?*

The son says, *Nothing.*

The dad asks, *Is that so?*

The son says, *Yes.*

The dad asks, *How do you come to that conclusion?*

The son says, *With practice.*

Comprehension

One night I looked at my cat and found I had the ability to comprehend language the way it was intended instead of what was actually said. In meows I could tell he was saying, *I care not for your existence.* When my wife said, *It's fine,* I knew what she meant was, *I need more help.* I texted my best friend, *I miss you,* and he sent me back *Same, bro,* which I somehow knew meant *I want to say I love you but can't without too much consternation on my part...It's just the way I was raised.* I tried to apply my newfound power retroactively to the things my father used to say, and I came to some startling conclusions. I found that his words were untranslatable, that the memories of his utterances defied my power and I had to make up what he meant based on what he said, which meant that I had to inhabit his mind, which meant that I had to get progressively drunker and meaner. And I didn't want to do that. My power, as it turned out, was short-lived.

Funeral

I'm in the habit of imagining my father's funeral. I wonder how well it will be attended, whether the food at the wake will be healthy or not. I'm not necessarily imagining his death, just his funeral. And it's a fetid sort of thought process, a winding staircase of disappointment in the way you can't effectively mourn the dead you barely know past a certain point. And cascading from all this is the choice of whether or not to go, which suit to wear, which human face to adorn. I keep a lineup of them in my closet and try them on from time to time, in anticipation of the event. One is a smile dripping upward, the product of eating a favorite meal, the perfect fit for photographs. Another a mask of grief, perfectly proportioned for maximum sadness, beautiful in its own way, the way it will look to all the other onlookers – the broken son staring in remembrance. And still there are more, countless more faces, in progressively shaded rows, that will never be considered.

Needles

After the medication change, I became obsessed with needles. Especially their thinness, the slight curvature of some. I became obsessed with indentations in the back of my hand, flirting with the edge of hurt, the memory of hospital beds and blood draws. The insertion of a peripheral catheter after a tooth infection darkened my mouth. The new meds made me crave needles of all shapes, and I went to the craft store to buy pincushions and boxes of needles, some with gaudy colored tips. My wife started to complain that they were a danger to our toddler son. So I stored them in the attic and switched to getting tattoos. The constant jabbing and bleeding fed the want. Before long both my arms were covered, and I lost track of the wounds. I kept taking the medicine, and eventually the obsession waned, but from time to time, I still feel the streaming desire for more pain.

Shrink

My son keeps getting smaller. One day, he's the size of a tumbler glass. The next, a bouncy ball. My wife and I take turns holding him in our palms, holding him up to the light to make sure he's still there. We buy microscopes just to be prepared, always have a magnifying glass on hand. We take him to the doctor, who says it's just a phase, that it'll all work out in the end. But we're not so sure. When he's the size of a single water droplet, we're convinced that we'll lose him for good. I'm watching him nestle into the creases of my right hand, wave my magnifying glass over top to check for the faintest hint of breath. Even as I hold him, he feels impossibly far away, trapped somewhere. When I can't stand the weightlessness of his tiny form, I pass him to my wife, who holds him up to her mouth.

Writer

When I sit down to write about my father, the wind picks up and whistles through the windows. The words spiral out of my fingers without context, lacking in some way that can only be explained by his absence, the memory of his voice lodged in my chest. I come back to page with only the gauzy memories of bourbon on his breath, a hand wrapped around my upper arm, him sprinting across a soccer field. When I sit down to write about my father, every single bad thing that could happen seems on the verge of happening. A car goes careening into the guardrail on a flyover ramp. Waves buckle under the pressure of shaking earth and rip toward shore. My son jumps out of his crib. I separate my shoulder for the fourth time, go back to sticking my finger down my throat. When I sit down to write about my father, I wonder what he meant by all the countless utterances of to be fair, if that were code for *I need you to know something about how fundamentally disappointing you are*. At least that's how I interpret it.

Crow

The crow is a strange and beautiful bird. It was my father's favorite animal, and he'd still shoot it off the fencepost given the chance.

Translation

I love you more than anything in this world = I own you
You're my best friend = Please, please don't ever lose me
You know that, right? = You cannot deny me
Please, stop = How could you do this to me?

Mercy

Inside my father's safe there is a forest of broken pines. Inside the forest of broken pines there is a letter written to me. Inside the letter written to me there is a wet heart. Inside the wet heart there is an orchid. Inside the orchid there is a grasping hand. Inside the grasping hand there is a shot of bourbon. Inside the shot of bourbon there is a concrete goose wearing a bonnet. Inside the concrete goose wearing a bonnet there is my only memory of my grandfather. Inside the only memory of my grandfather there is a plastic tumbler. Inside the plastic tumbler there is a solitary frog. Inside the solitary frog there is a headlamp. Inside the headlamp there is an urn. Inside the urn there is a mattress lying by the creek. Inside the mattress lying by the creek there is my father's pistol. Inside my father's pistol there is a flip flop covered in sand. Inside the flip flop covered in sand there is a fractured tibia. Inside the fractured tibia there is a gallon of milk. Inside the gallon of milk there is my son's toy truck. Inside my son's toy truck there is forgiveness.

Drink

Refusal is the right of the son when yet another cocktail is forced on him by his father. This is the rite of summer nights and the ritual of best friends getting loaded by the pond. Cattails swaying, a dragonfly resting on the rim of the sweating glass. But the refusal never comes. It's just more drink and harangue, habits forming early. The son sixteen. The father older than he has any right to be. And it's the confusion of sloughed skin that rectifies the drunken haze, the future of an aching jaw, the memory of being put on the ground just a few nights ago on one like this – a night where the stars and rippling water sit undefined by anything other than their consumption.

Song of the Father

It begins with a ball of light dropping into the stomach, the blinding spin as it lodges. It ends with a boy's odyssey out of childhood and into fatherhood, more spinning. In between, there are 280 characters online talking about sports, five hundred utterances of the same phrase over and over, portraits on the page. In between, there are hands cloaked in bile, horns sprouting out the sides of the head, fits thrown at first base and at the side of a judo contest area. There is Shiai. There are the rare instances of compassion, of naked sharing, of unbroken promise gliding out of a wounded throat. There is the pile of forever growing ever larger in the back forty.

Song of the Son

Song of the son leaking out of the cicada, billowing on the breeze. Slight modifications to the beat to fit the father, who stalks the territory of his own making, making a rut on the fenceline with his hooves. The father is half-man-half-goat and all bile, searching for the source. Song of the son booming under the tent of night, ringing off the starlight and sliding down the throat, rattling the ribcage. And then there's the father slinking along with his cloven feet, his leaning gait and sanguine tongue tasting the air, getting closer. Song of the son ripping through the layers of regret and languid attempts at apologia, sticking in the craw of the father who can't bring himself to transform back, who can't bring his own form to level out in the fescue and just lie down for something other than sex with someone other than his wife. The father skulking away, defeated and burning with a heart lit on fire, horns ablaze, filled with the song of his son catching in his mouth.

Mandates

Don't forget about the sweeping silence of knees scraped, the aftermath of a tumble. Come around for the important events, even if you've screwed them up in the past, and be sure to leave a snakeskin by the door for luck. Remember how to father, how to roll over and expose your stomach, how to blow out the candles. Accept the revisions proposed by the son and hold them up to the chandelier to check for holes. Verify the results of previous encounters, especially the ones that ended up with one of you on their back screaming. Complete the cycle by careening through the back door with apologies tattooed on your wrist, with the words already rehearsed and sudden on the tongue, with a backwoods scent spilling out of your mouth along with the words, with all your ducks in a row, with the calligraphy of sidestepping the indiscretion hot on your trail. Come with a blinding resplendence in your bones ready to light up the night; come with a rock in your fist, ready to drop to show you're standing down. Be the father you always wanted to be, the one with a velvet hand and thundering voice, the one without a slip of a tongue into another's mouth, the one who stayed and never left.

Worlds

There's a world pinned in the palm of my father's hand, a whole world replete with shades of long-lost families he never had anything to do with and families he will leave us for in the future. I know this because I've seen the little orb spinning in his palm, the utter brilliance of it, the way he thinks it's hidden. The dark heaviness of it. The ghostly touch, the wizened fingertips of others reaching for his cavernous mouth, the way our family seems to smudge in the mirror the longer he holds it. I know this because I've held the world myself, flirted with the edge of another and licked the tantalizing salt of desire slathered on an earlobe, the other world, this one, the one that can't be held, tilting wildly. I chose to give the little world back to my father, chose my wife, my son.

Fire

Sometimes I imagine the renovation of soul. How I might pack up a set of fine tools and poke around, chip away, steal the shavings of self. How the entire act may be clandestine, as though trying to hide from fate lurking in the creases of my fingers. Or it might be brazen, a bare-knuckled dismantling of a slab of memory that will pass into the roiling ocean concealed in my throat. In each case, the polishing of desire might reflect itself in the dappled remembrance of a father's touch. I think to myself as I work that, perhaps, where there's smoke, there really is fire, and that fire is so hot it may burn the very walls I'm brushing. That it may ignite being and let it emerge, slick and wind-whipped. With fire, there are two guarantees – it burns up and down. But incineration is part of the process of becoming the son. Then again, I suppose I can stop whenever, can decide never to begin.

Discussion Guide

by

Tiffany Woodley

1. Luke Wortley begins the collection with a poem entitled "Expecting." Given the rest of the book, why does he choose to start readers here?

2. Many of these poems center on the complexity of the speaker both longing for a relationship with his father and refusing to connect. Where were these moments most clear for you? Which seems to be more weighted in the speaker's mind?

3. Poems such as "Near Miss", "Stairs", "Monster" and "Shrink" (among others) feel very surreal in nature. How does the author use the surreal to make a realistic point? How does using this angle embellish these scenes?

4. Though the speaker distances himself from his father, he also seems to hold some of the same traits. Where do the two men overlap? How do they differ? You may want to consult some of the paired poems with "son" and "father" as part of this process.

5. In "Mandates", the poet shifts to an instructional tone, speaking directly to the father. What is Wortley's purpose in his approach to this poem?

6. Though the collection is entirely prose poems, Wortley does play with structure at a few different moments such as in "Conversation" and "What Happens When We Die." How do these unique pieces stand out?

7. In "Funeral", Wortley wonders "which human face to adorn" at his father's funeral. What do his options suggest about how the speaker feels? When are other times in life when there are many options like this on the face one wears?

8. "Language", "Translation", and "Comprehension" each deal with the speaker attempting to understand his father's perspective. What is this journey like? Where does the journey leave him?

9. In "Box", Wortley speaks about carrying memories with him in a cardboard box. How does the means of transport inform our understanding of these memories? What would you hold were you to carry your own?

10. Poems including "Four Wheeler" and "Pocket Square" lean into descriptive language and the setting in particular. How does the poet's use of description impact the narratives of these poems?

11. "Bones" and "The Early Days" each repeat a word through while "Beast" repeats words back to back (called anadiplosis). Return to these poems with an eye to the impact these repetitions have on the sound and meaning within these pieces.

12. In one poem, the writer mentions that "I am obsessed with throats." At various points in the collection, Wortley shows this to be true including acts of bulimia, silence brewing within, as well as taking medicine and liquor. What are the purposes that throats serve in this volume? What is spoken and what is left unsaid?

Acknowledgements

Special thanks to the following publications and their editorial staffs for accepting versions of these poems:

"Father in War Time," "The Son Holds," and "Call" – *Pithead Chapel*
"Cry" and "Dad's Weekend" – *Cincinnati Review*
"Orchids" and "Tumbler" – *Threadcount*
"Expecting" – *Unbroken Journal*
"Monster" – *HAD*
"Goatman" – *Club Plum Literary Journal*
"Stairs" and "Church" – *[sub]liminal magazine*
"Beast" – *Trampset*
"The Early Days" – *Chestnut Review*
"Footsweep" – *Cobra Milk*
"Funeral" – *Coffin Bell Journal*
"Patrilineal" – *Not Deer Magazine.*
"Ouroboros," "Conversation," "Comprehension," and "Mercy" – *Cutleaf*
"Sunflower" – *Kissing Dynamite*

First, an inadequate but nevertheless sincere thank you to Karen Cline-Tardiff and Jennifer Taylor, the twin pillars of Gnashing Teeth Publishing. Y'all took a chance on this strange work, and I will be forever grateful.

Thank you to my mom, Theresa Wortley, and to my sibling, Nat Wortley, for always being there. I don't know what else to say.

To Katelin Rice, my wonderful and beautiful partner. You are my role model, my best friend. You have never wavered. This book is also partially for you.

Thank you as well to the fictioneers: Laura Todd, Leslie Walker Trahan, Zeke Cork, and Julie Watson. I don't know how I could've completed a single project without you.

To my friends, professors, and peers: Logan Spackman, Earl Carrender, Allie Field Bell, Grant Catton, Storm Humbert, Colt Humbert, Ian Gibson, Chris Speckman, Brady Allen, Madeleine Corley, Christopher McCurry, Todd Dillard, Robert Vaughan, Leigh Chadwick, Roy G. Guzmán, Eduardo C. Corral, Susan Sutherlin, Robin Arble, Ross White, William Erickson, Frances Klein, and Susan Neville. This book carries the ghosts of all your words that you've ever said or typed to me about writing and life in general. I appreciate every one of them as my little hauntings hopefully do justice to your influence.

Additional thanks goes out to Ben Niespodziany, Taylor Byas, Jose Hernandez Diaz, and Michael Martone. The time you spent with this work was invaluable, and I hope I can repay you someday.

The Books & Brews Mothership in Indianapolis, IN also deserves a heap of gratitude for being my writing sanctuary and general safe spot over the years.

One more special shoutout to The Red Cloaks and all my gaming buddies I've made over the years bonding over cardboard on the table. You have been an intellectual and emotional support system from afar always.

Without all your unbridled support, generosity, and consistent love for me and my work, none of this would be possible.

About The Author

Luke is originally from Simpsonville, KY, and his beloved Bluegrass State features prominently in his work.

He has a BA in Spanish from Wright State University and an MFA from Butler University, where he was the former fiction editor of *Booth: A Journal*. After a few years in high schools as a graduate assistant, volunteer, and ultimately a Spanish teacher, he began working for a population and public health not-for-profit as a grant writer and a program director for community outreach among under-served populations. Luke has also been an adjunct professor at Butler University teaching Latin American history and First Year Seminar. He writes short fiction, flash variants, and prose poetry.

He lives in Indianapolis with his partner, children, dog, and cats.